'Interesting, clear and a fun read. A book that challenges you to question and think deeper into life and faith. With practical application and questions to reflect up[illegible] ing people, you [illegible] ow more about [illegible] nd Jesus applic[illegible] ook to read but [illegible] op.'

Gemma Symonds, Youth Pastor – Life Church Bedworth, UK

'Tired of scrolling? Looking for a new adventure and experience that makes the digital world seem boring? Are you hungry to know the truth? Audacious as it may seem, if you pick up this book you'll find the answer to the searching and longing of your soul, you'll find purpose and a reason to live, and you'll discover adventure beyond your wildest dreams. Believe it or not, it's found in following Jesus. That's my story, and it is true for billions of others worldwide so why not read Like or Follow *now and find out why Jesus is not just a big deal, he's the only One worth exploring. Warning, it may change your life!'*

Josh Green, Youth Director – 24-7 Prayer

'Curiosity is key to your future – the questions you have, the interest in your mind, and the stirring in your heart – allow these to take you on a journey with this book to discover life, purpose, and hope for the future.'

Dan Randall, YxYA Director – HOPE Together

'Like or Follow *gently takes the reader on a journey of 'Why?' With thought-provoking questions to consider at the end of each chapter and short video clips to access via a QR code, the author presents opportunities for the reader to explore what faith in Jesus offers us in the context of our life experiences.'*

Matthew Foster, Director – Engage Trust UK

'I've never read such clear messaging about what it means to be a Christian and how to think through what I believe and why. I've always shared my parents' faith, and that's been great, but this book has helped me confidently take ownership of my journey. It feels like the author really understands the struggles and thoughts of teens and how to make complex ideas easily understandable.'

Nina Johnston, aged 14, USA

LIKE
OR
FOLLOW

WHAT EVERY TEENAGER NEEDS TO DECIDE ABOUT JESUS

DAVE BODEN

10 Publishing
a division of 10 of those.com

This book is dedicated to all those who have helped me discover Jesus for myself.

British Library Cataloguing in Publication Data
A record for this book is available from the British Library

ISBN: 978-1-914966-97-2

Designed and typeset by Pete Barnsley (CreativeHoot.com)

All videos used courtesy of www.kleerseries.com

Printed in the UK

10Publishing, a division of 10ofthose.com
Unit C, Tomlinson Road, Leyland, PR25 2DY, England

Email: info@10ofthose.com
Website: www.10ofthose.com

3 5 7 10 8 6 4 2

CONTENTS

INTRODUCTION

RETHINK?

Curiosity has earned a bad reputation ever since it apparently killed a cat. So well done for being interested enough to pick up this book and read it past the first sentence. Let's start with the basics: Yes, this is a book about Jesus Christ. It would be easy to stop here, dismissing this as some sort of religious waffle that won't have any significant impact on your life.

But think about this for a second.

Nearly a third of the world's population believes Jesus has changed the world. That's over 2.2

billion people! His significance is not limited to people of a certain country, race, or background. Jesus is followed by those of all nationalities and ethnicities; by the rich, poor, young, and old. This crosses borders and boundaries like nothing else. Interest in him is not just limited to those who follow Christianity either. Muslims, Hindus, Buddhists, and many other religions all believe something about him, even if they don't always agree on who Jesus is. In fact, he's easily the most famous person in history.

So, before you write Jesus off, wouldn't it at least be worth considering why so many people follow him? You don't have to be from a religious background to learn about Jesus. And even if you are, it's good to explore more about what you really think for yourself.

You may have noticed that some people like to buy fake designer items online to show off to their friends. They are often such good copies that it can be hard to tell them apart from the real thing – for a while. The fake stuff may not cost very much, but it never lasts long. When it comes to deciding what you really think about

Jesus, you may find it easy to fake belief because you feel a bit of pressure from someone else. Maybe you want to please your parents, or you know a group of people who are keen for you to believe what they do. But if you want this journey to last longer than five minutes, then you have to decide you will not fake it for others, but do it for real for yourself.

I have no idea where the British rapper Stormzy is on his spiritual journey, but he once explained how we've each got to think for ourselves:

> *'We grew up in church. I've had faith all my life. I've loved God all my life. But I feel like you've got to come to your own realisation.'*[1]

Hopefully, this book will help you come to your own conclusion.

Before we jump in, let me tell you a little about how the book is structured. We will look at six big themes together:

---

1 Stormzy, Louis Theroux Interviews, BBC, 2022

1. Jesus is relevant: Christ provides us with what we're really looking for.
2. Jesus is real: History proves that Christ was a real person who made a real difference.
3. Jesus is God's reflection: Christ shows us exactly what God is like and reminds us who we really are.
4. Jesus is a rescuer: Christ saves us by dying for us.
5. Jesus is a revolutionary: We are invited to join Christ's purpose to bring hope.
6. Jesus offers you a relationship: When you put your trust in Christ, he will be with you forever.

At the end of each section, there are questions to reflect on, either by yourself or with someone you trust. You can also watch a video to hear a recap of the topic.

As you read you may come across a short quote from the Bible like this one:

> *'For this is how God loved the world: He gave his one and only Son, so that everyone who believes in him will not perish but have eternal life.'* **John 3:16**

The section in bold refers to the part of the Bible the quote is taken from. Need to know how to find a Bible verse? **John 3:16** = the Bible book 'John', chapter 3 (the big numbers in each Bible book) and verse 16 (the small numbers in each chapter).

As you finish the book, you will be given a series of choices regarding what to do next. Avoid spoilers and don't skip to the end just yet!

You can kick start your own journey of discovery right now. Everyone is welcome.

LET'S GO.

1

RELEVANT?

OVERCOME A BAD FIRST IMPRESSION OF JESUS BY BECOMING CURIOUS

There are some awkward ways someone on a first date could make a bad impression. They'd crash and burn if they only talked about themselves; or even worse, if they hardly spoke at all because they were too consumed by live streaming updates to their mates! They're unlikely to get a second date – first impressions matter too much.

This is not just true for the dating game.

I heard a story about a young person who went for his first job interview at a large superstore. Midway through, the interviewer was called outside for five minutes to deal with a customer service issue. When he returned, the teenager was fast asleep, sprawled out across the desk of the boss! He didn't land the job. Here's a top tip for if you ever go for a job interview… have a nap before you go!

First impressions can last a long time.

Have you ever felt judged by someone who didn't actually know the real you? It sucks, right? Nobody enjoys being misunderstood or stereotyped based on scraps of information rather than the whole picture. Yet, we do this to other people all the time. We often form opinions on others based on information that isn't valid at all. We so easily judge a book by its cover.

Here's another thing to consider about first impressions: Can we really trust outward appearances? Experts say that the reason con men are so successful is that they know how to give people a false impression. They might show you warmth, trust, and attention on the outside, but secretly they're out to trick you. People fall for their schemes because they make judgments in a split second based on initial feelings, rather than concrete facts.

It's so important we don't just look at life with a shallow perspective.

First impressions can hold us back in getting to know a person for who they really are. Ask yourself how many times you've had an opinion about someone that has turned out not to be true? Most people have at least one friend who they didn't think much of, or even disliked at the start, but later turned out to be one of their besties!

It's only when you get curious enough to take that second look that you're reminded there's so much more going on beneath the surface.

THREE TYPES OF JESUS

Jesus may be a well-known figure from history, yet, when you hear his name, you might not have a burning desire to follow in his footsteps.

He might seem pretty irrelevant to your life right now. But what if that's just because you've had a bad first impression of him?

Maybe you only recognise 'Jesus Christ' as a phrase thrown around as a swear word. Perhaps when you think about that name, you immediately associate it with ideas of a dry, boring religion. Or you've googled 'Jesus' and discovered millions of ancient images that aren't exactly on point with the latest trend.

There seem to be three types of Christ we come across when we scroll through social media or search online. There's Jesus the joke, Jesus the Jedi, and Jesus the judge.

First up is Jokey Jesus.

The vast majority of pictures we see online make Christ the butt of everyone's jokes. We see countless memes of him giving us a winking smile and a jolly thumbs up. Elsewhere, we find Jesus dressed in various types of sports gear, chatting to celebrities and cartoon characters, or even riding on the back of a dinosaur! It's interesting that 2,000 years before a single image was shared on a group chat, Jesus was already being mocked by people that completely misunderstood him. Because he hung out with individuals most people considered corrupt, he was labelled a greedy drunk. When he was arrested and crucified, many made fun of him for claiming to be from God. Dismissing Jesus as a joke is clearly not a new idea.

Next up is Jedi Jesus.

If you have ever visited an art gallery, you may have seen religious images of Jesus with a long, flowing mysterious robe that makes him look just like Obi-Wan Kenobi. If you gave this Jesus a lightsaber, then he may as well be a member of the Rebel Alliance! Why would anyone be interested in a guy who walks around wearing sandals and sporting a white dressing gown and long flowing hair?

The funny thing is that even this artistic impression of Jesus is completely made up. Clearly, they didn't have cameras back then, but even without the benefit of photographic evidence, we know Jesus was a brown-skinned,

Middle-Eastern man, not a blond, white-skinned, all-American hero. So, if the pictures we see of Jesus from the past are not even accurate, no wonder they're not making you rush to fit him into the picture of your future.

Finally, there is Judgey Jesus.

This is the version of Christ that looks like he's on the warpath and out to spoil everyone's fun. He's often associated with harsh quotes and comes across as full of anger and prejudice. Sadly, there are many that see Christ's followers in exactly the same way. The idea of a judgemental community that serves a judgemental God is not very appealing to anyone.

If we default to thinking he's just a happy joke, a hippy Jedi, or a harsh judge, then we will always underestimate the real Jesus.

A MAN WORTH KNOWING

Here's the thing: 2,000 years ago, if you tried to say that Jesus was irrelevant to his friends, or even to his enemies, they would have dismissed you as a terrible judge of character. The real Jesus always caused a reaction.

Jesus was known for being adventurous, thought-provoking, and inspirational. You either loved him because of the way he treated you, or hated him because of how he challenged your life. He was branded by some as a rebel and others as a rescuer; and yet nobody ever accused him of being bland!

This was a man who was loving, compassionate, and kind. The people around him felt cared for in a way that few had encountered at the time – or that we might experience, even today. He always treated everyone like they had equal value and worth. In behaving this way, it's said that Jesus revealed the true heart of God for all of us.

The real Jesus made a lasting impression.

It wasn't just his personality that made people want to take a second look at him. His words still powerfully resonate with people all over the world today. For example, the simple phrase, 'Do to others whatever you would like them to do to you', found in **Matthew 7:12**, is the foundation of our modern laws. You may even hear it spoken about in the school classroom as the 'golden rule' of how to treat each other.

At a time when fear and anxiety was impacting mental health, just like today, Christ taught people how to find peace by focusing on God's love:

> *'Look at the birds. They don't plant or harvest or store food in barns, for your heavenly Father feeds them. And aren't you far more valuable to him than they are? Can all your worries add a single moment to your life?'* **Matthew 6:26–27**

A lot of what Jesus spoke about seems to go against the grain of what we hear from celebrities, influencers, and voices in popular culture right now. For example, they tend to be quick to judge, or try to cancel those who think differently from them, but Jesus had a different approach:

> *'Do not judge others, and you will not be judged. Do not condemn others, or it will all come back against you. Forgive others, and you will be forgiven.'* **Luke 6:37**

Jesus reminded us that life has a purpose worth discovering, fame is not always worth following, and money is not the only goal worth pursuing. He asked his followers:

> *'And what do you benefit if you gain the whole world but lose your own soul?'* **Mark 8:36**

You couldn't imagine the latest social media influencer broadcasting live from their multi-millionaire mansion and declaring something like that! Jesus said these words and more. However, just because his claims are different, that doesn't mean they're not worth looking into. These are ideas that have stood the test of time. His message is worth so much more than a meme.

A LIFE WORTH FOLLOWING

In the Bible, there are so many stories of people who met Jesus and were changed for the better when they became curious about who he really was. Peter was a young fisherman who felt like his future was all mapped out. Unlike maybe a few of his friends, academic success hadn't come, and he ended up assuming his whole life would revolve around the family fishing business. Then he met Jesus for the first time and began to get a taste of adventure. What if his life could be about something more?

Jesus took ordinary people like Peter and called them to a higher purpose. He helped them see who they really were, and what they could do with their lives. Peter went from a speak-before-engaging-brain man who more often than not put his foot in it, to a humble yet strong leader who taught thousands.

I still hear stories about those who encounter Jesus for the first time, and how it changes everything for them. I have a YouTuber friend, who has well over 100k subscribers on her channel. Nowadays, she travels all over the world sharing stories about her real-life experience of knowing Jesus, but it wasn't always like that.

Her hard-hitting story starts with a girl desperate to find out who she was from a young age. As a child, she had been to church but decided it wasn't relevant to her life and never gave it another thought when she hit her teenage years.

In one of her YouTube videos, she explains how she was on an endless quest to find her sense of identity and self-worth. Whether through constantly collecting guys' phone numbers or wearing revealing clothes to make herself feel valued by the attention, she hoped that, 'if I did certain things, people would see me and say, I want to be her friend'.

Her life spiralled into a cycle of toxic relationships, underage drinking, smoking weed, and living the clubbing lifestyle using a fake ID. Although she presented a cool and confident impression on the outside, she often cried herself to sleep, and never quite felt good enough on the inside.

When her world eventually began falling apart, she suddenly thought about going back to church. It took a while but as she read more about the real Jesus in the Bible, and began praying to God, she felt her identity slowly change from the inside out. After finding security, forgiveness, love, and a sense of purpose, her life was never the same again.

- The Jesus she discovered was not a joke.
- The Jesus she discovered was not a fairy tale.
- The Jesus she discovered was not a harsh, angry judge.

Jesus left a lasting impression. This is just one story out of millions, and it's an example of what is still happening today; young people are being changed by Christ after they choose to follow him. So, to answer the question about whether Jesus is still relevant to you, you simply have to decide to become curious.

Start by asking yourself the question, what do you want out of your life?

- If you want to find out more about who you are…
- If you want to find out more about your purpose…
- If you want to figure out what you really need…
- If you want to find out more about what really matters…

… then Christ is definitely worth thinking twice about.

So, if your own first impression of Jesus hasn't been that great so far, why not take a second look.

> **'CHRIST PROVIDES US WITH WHAT WE ARE REALLY LOOKING FOR.'**

QUESTIONS TO THINK ABOUT:

- Can you think of a time when you had a wrong first impression of someone?
- What is the thing that you find most interesting about Jesus?
- Why might it be worth you taking a second look at who Jesus is?

WATCH THIS VIDEO:

2

REAL?

ESTABLISH THE FACTS ABOUT JESUS FOR YOURSELF

It wasn't so long ago that we only had to worry about whether UFOs, aliens, or the Loch Ness Monster were fake news. But looking at the latest crazy headlines, it's hard to figure out if anything is genuine anymore.

Here are a couple of real-life newspaper articles that seem mad but are in fact true…

- 'Police called in over killer goldfish.'

- 'Fire crew called in after smoke seen in sky – turned out to be a cloud.'
- 'Student who electrocuted his nipples sues teacher… for not warning him it was dangerous.'

I am not sure where to start with those (especially that last one). Truth is often stranger than fiction, which is why it's so hard to tell the difference. Nowadays, a fake story will go viral and fly around the world before anyone realises it's been made up. Stories often contain just enough bits of twisted truth to convince you not to bother to look behind the headlines.

People share fake news for different motives. They may want to make money out of you by getting more clicks on a webpage, or promote their ideas to influence you, or simply because they want to trick you and have fun at your expense.

The rise of fact-checking websites like Snopes mean, if we want to, we can now go to great lengths to double-check everything that's said or shared to determine if it's factual. You are encouraged to check the source, look for obvious errors, see if others can confirm the story, and make sure the picture you are being painted reflects what happened.

So, with figuring out the existence of a historical person like Jesus Christ, how on earth can we know if we're talking about real history or an ancient myth? What can you prove about someone who supposedly lived over 2,000 years ago in the Middle East?

Some people say Jesus was a made-up figure based on lots of other types of classical heroes. What then if Jesus turns out to be faker than your friend's new Gucci bag? Couldn't that basically mean that the whole of Christianity was born out of a prank that went viral? But no serious investigator would say that stacks up. Loads of people disagree about who he was, but very few go as far as saying he didn't exist.

There's a story about an investigative journalist called Lee Strobel who was sceptical about whether there was enough evidence to prove Jesus was an actual historical person. After doing loads of research, he discovered the opposite was true. He found you could establish the facts and evidence about Christ in a court of law with much more certainty than a lot of other figures in history. You may want to go and read a copy of Strobel's book *The Case for Christ: Young Readers Edition* if you are interested in exploring in more detail.

Strobel figured out that you don't need to wade through receipts, phone records, or CCTV footage to know if a historical figure existed. We obviously can't check Jesus' online profile. But we can mark a distinct point in history when his followers started talking about him all over the place. And those conversations left their mark in history.

FACT OR FICTION?

The life of Jesus triggered a massive download, not of pics, posts and memes, but of writing, letters and documents. Four of Jesus' friends, Matthew, Mark, Luke, and John, shared their messages widely amongst the very communities they came from, so they could have been easily exposed as fake news. There were names of real people and real places, many you can still visit. They wrote about recent events that others could check out by talking to people who were also there. If what they wrote was false, it could have easily been dismissed. Yet the stories stuck.

For example, a man called Luke wrote an account of the events surrounding Jesus to his friend Theophilus so that he had a record of what was going on. He started his letter by saying:

> *'Many people have set out to write accounts about the events that have been fulfilled among us. They used the eyewitness reports circulating among us from the early disciples. Having carefully investigated everything from the beginning, I also have decided to write an accurate account for you, most honourable Theophilus, so you can be certain of the truth of everything you were taught.'* **Luke 1:1–4**

Jesus' followers drew from their own first-hand experience of being with him so that what was written came out of a personal encounter and not just second-hand information:

> *'... We saw him with our own eyes and touched him with our own hands...'* **1 John 1:1**

This written evidence came not just from those who were fans of Jesus, either. Ancient historians like Josephus and Tacitus, who were not part of Jesus' crew, confirmed details of his life. Some of those writing about Jesus didn't like him. They accused him of being a magic man and leading people into stupid ideas, but they never denied his existence. One Roman called Pliny even wrote letters that spoke with great pleasure about arresting some of the early Christians just for fun. What a loser!

This raises another point: Many of the first followers of Christ faced the prospect of terrible deaths if they remained Christians. But those who claimed to have met Jesus didn't renounce their story and save their own skins by saying 'Only joking!' Why would they bother fabricating all this if they knew it was fake? It wouldn't get them a special prize or an easier life. In fact, the opposite was true. Within a few years of Christianity spreading, the Roman Emperor Nero burned Christians to death or threw them to the lions! Still, Christ's followers didn't relent.

I don't know many people who would give up their real life for fake news, do you?

And what has been written is so interesting because many of the stories about Jesus don't exactly paint his followers in a perfect light. Nowadays, we like to edit our lives on social media to show only the best parts.

- We show everyone the sunset on the beach but not the rainy weather that follows.
- We highlight the perfect coffee latte art, but not the spills or stains that made it happen.
- We post the one time we smash our personal record, yet delete the thousand times we fail.

We rarely reveal the rough bits behind the scenes. Yet the stories about Christ hide little. They tell it, warts and all. His followers record the mistakes they made and the arguments they had with each other. They report the stupid things that were said and the times they got it wrong. When it all kicked off and Jesus was killed, his friends ran away and denied they even knew him. There was no attempt to cover any of this up. If you were going to invent a story about some fictional guy who changed the world, then why would you make yourself look like an idiot when you were doing it?

FAKE OR TRUE?

Archaeologists have been able to back up many of the details talked about in the Bible. One example is an inscription on an ancient stone discovered in 1961 that proves details about who the Bible says was governor at the time of Jesus.[2] This provides evidence that what the Bible says is accurate.

Another example is where experts have uncovered the ruins of the Pool of Siloam, a place where Jesus is said to have performed a miracle. Some had previously claimed it wasn't a real location, but while excavating a sewage works in 2004, builders found the exact shape

2 Bryan Windle, 'Pontius Pilate: An Archaeological Biography', (11 Oct 2019), *Bible Archaeology Report* https://biblearchaeologyreport.com/2019/10/11/pontius-pilate-an-archaeological-biography/ [assessed 14 June 2023]

and details of the pool. Then they discovered coins that fixed the date of the pool to the time of Jesus.[3] The evidence adds up.

They say that you can tell a lot about a ship by the wake it leaves behind in the water. In the same way, Jesus left some pretty big waves in our world! Before Jesus, there were no churches, zero Christians, and Christianity was non-existent. But then there was a massive explosion of all these at a very specific point in the timeline of history. It was like an earthquake hit over 2,000 years ago and the shock waves are still being felt around the world.

How else could you explain this away other than by accepting it actually happened?

The very mention of the term 'Christian' on public record so soon after Jesus was around is a massive sign that someone really had come on the scene. A Christian was a follower of Christ. You wouldn't have Swifties without Taylor

---

3 'Ancient Pool of Siloam to be Excavated and Opened to the Public', (27 Dec 2022), *Israeli Government website* https://www.gov.il/en/departments/news/pool-of-siloam-to-be-excavated-and-opened-to-the-public-27-dec-2022 [assessed 14 June 2023]

Swift. There wouldn't be Beliebers without an actual Justin Bieber. And you certainly wouldn't have Christians without there being someone called Jesus Christ!

History has confirmed so many things about Jesus: He lived as a travelling preacher, died on a cross, and his tomb was empty three days after he died. After his death, you would expect things to calm down, but that's when things go viral. His followers claimed Jesus came back to life! Over 500 witnesses claimed to have seen him in the flesh. Even people who previously hadn't believed in Jesus admitted they had seen him alive again after his death. Some people think thieves stole his body, but what if only rising from the dead could have sparked the sudden rise of the faith known as Christianity?

Christ's life has been deemed so significant that even today's date is determined by the year of his birth. If this man really is part of our history, then that probably gives us some questions to consider for our future.

'HISTORY PROVES THAT CHRIST WAS A REAL PERSON WHO MADE A REAL DIFFERENCE.'

QUESTIONS TO THINK ABOUT:

- What does the idea that Jesus is real mean to you?
- What is the most interesting evidence for the existence of Jesus you have read about in this chapter?
- Why do you think Jesus' existence is so important?

WATCH THIS VIDEO:

3

REFLECTION?

FOCUS YOUR ATTENTION ON WHO JESUS IS AND DISCOVER WHAT GOD IS REALLY LIKE

What image springs to your mind when you first think about God? Do you picture an old man on a white cloud, or an impersonal energy like the Force in Star Wars? Perhaps you see a powerful creator, an angry dictator, or just a distant spectator? We all have an image of God that often comes from the things we see around us.

This might be the first time you have even thought about God in your entire life, but you wouldn't be the first person to do so. Many have looked far and wide simply to decide there is no God at all. When people look at the world, they see no evidence of a creator anywhere. Some people conclude that God can't possibly be real because you can't see him in front of your face.

But wait a sec. Just because you cannot see something doesn't mean it's not real right? Every time we turn on a light switch, we rely on electricity, even though we can't see it. Every time a tree sways during a storm, we see the effects of the wind. We never see germs, but you wouldn't have so many runny noses without them.

We see the impact of invisible things all the time.

Invisible things really matter too. They matter to the astronaut who counts every unit of the unseen air he breathes as his rocket leaves the Earth's atmosphere. And they matter to the rock climber who needs ropes and a harness in case she slips, knowing unseen gravity will pull her down. The things we can't see are just as important as the things we can.

There's an old illustration that goes something like this: Imagine you are walking along a beach and you come across a gold watch. You pick it up and see the dials, the gears, and the intricate pieces perfectly formed to tell the time. As you look at this beautifully crafted item, you think about how it got there and how it was made. Perhaps it came into being by total chance: The waves of the shore bashed back and forth on the sand, and slowly, somehow, over millions of years, the watch formed itself from nothing and ticked. The second option is more straightforward. You conclude there was a watchmaker.

This story makes us ask questions about whether we were made on purpose. Are we like a computer that switched itself on after accidentally building itself from microchips that appeared from nowhere? Or was there a designer? The Bible points out that God proves his own existence, not just by the way he designed humans, but in how the whole world was made:

> *'For ever since the world was created, people have seen the earth and sky. Through everything God made, they can clearly see his invisible*

> *qualities – his eternal power and divine nature. So they have no excuse for not knowing God.'*
> **Romans 1:20**

Want to prove the existence of God? Simply look outside. Or better still, go look in a mirror. You are the evidence. If you end up concluding that there is a God, then the next obvious question is, how do we know what God is like?

JESUS SHOWS US WHO GOD REALLY IS

Have you ever seen those mirror mazes at a theme park or creepy old fairground? There's often a moment in action films when the hero gets chased around and ends up running into their own reflection. That's the trick these mazes play on you! You look left, right, straight ahead, and behind, but it all looks the same.

Discovering who God is can feel just as disorientating.

Some people invent a God that conveniently mirrors themselves. Their creator talks like them, thinks like them, and wants the same things they want! It's safe to say, if your God has the same likes and dislikes as you; then you are basically bumping into your own reflection.

Others decide what God is like based on their background, culture, or nationality. This can get confusing. Consider how many interpretations you can end up with, depending on where you live and what others tell you to believe.

People have always been confused by the endless different answers to the question, 'Who is God?' It's almost like we're searching for a way out of that confusing mirror maze, but keep getting lost. It's so hard to find a way through.

So how do we stop getting lost in a thousand versions of God? Is there a compass to help us chart a way through?

> *'Jesus told him, "I am the way, the truth, and the life..."'* **John 14:6**

Apparently, the trick to navigating a mirror maze is to stop looking at the mirrors themselves. You've got to find a single point of reference to navigate your way through. Try that when you next live through an action movie sequence! Jesus made the shocking claim that he was that single point of reference for the whole of humanity.

Christians believe that if we want to know how God really thinks, speaks, and acts, then in Christ, we find the answer. Everything Jesus did reflected God's character.

> *'No one has ever seen God. But the unique One, who is himself God, is near to the Father's heart. He has revealed God to us.'* **John 1:18**

Because Jesus is loving, we know God is loving, too. Because of Jesus, we know that God wants to look after the lonely, care for the outcast, and bring hope for the future. The list of comparisons is endless.

> *'Christ is the visible image of the invisible God.'* **Colossians 1:15**

In other words, if God took a selfie, it would look like Jesus.

JESUS SHOWS US WHO WE ARE

Jesus doesn't just show us what God is like, he also reminds us who we are too.

Look around you and it's easy to see how much value we place on outward appearances to find our identity. We're so bombarded by images of perfection that it's very hard not to feel like a failure when we don't measure up to the media's impossible standards of what we're supposed to look or be like.

Advertising tries to make us believe messages like:

- Buy this stuff and you will be happy.
- Live this lifestyle and you will be free.
- Follow this social media account and you will belong.
- Get this job and you will be successful.

Here's what Jesus teaches as the alternative to what the world often says: You are *not* defined by your looks, the amount in your bank account, or the number on any scale. We are all equal regardless of who we are, where we are from, or the colour of our skin. Jesus came to remind you of your true identity and worth. You are made by God and loved by him.

> *'God showed how much he loved us by sending his one and only Son into the world so that we might have eternal life through him.'* **1 John 4:9**

Whenever we chase after things such as money, fame or power, none of it seems to last. We always end up wanting more and are never quite satisfied enough. The star of *Black Panther: Wakanda Forever*, Letitia Wright, has wrestled with this idea of never quite finding satisfaction in success. In one interview, she shares this about the challenges of being a young, famous woman growing up trying to find her identity:

> *'The world is so fickle, and there's not much that you can really put your hope in to make you feel whole. Even now I'm going through a new transformative stage of my life with understanding who I am, but with God, you can really just get through these situations. It's*

> *been beautiful to have my faith in Jesus, which is worth more than anything.'*[4]

We can clearly see here that Letitia embraces being loved by God.

There's a popular TV show called *The Voice.* The series involves wannabe pop stars that sing on a stage before a panel of judges who sit with their back to the contestants. In order to get their attention, they have to perform incredibly well and make the judges notice them. If they perform well enough and are talented enough, then a judge may choose them to the delight of a cheering audience. The red button is pressed, and the chair spins around, lighting up a big sign that says 'I WANT YOU'.

Many people think they have to get God's attention like this. They try to hustle, show off, and stand out to earn God's affection. Millions of people see themselves as unworthy. So, they work hard, give their best efforts, and perform a sort of 'song and a dance' trying to be better than

---

4 Quoted in Cara Bentley, 'Letitia Wright', Premier Christian News, 13 August 2021

everyone else, and somehow make themselves worthy of God's love.

But Jesus reminds us that God doesn't care if you are talented, gifted, or better than the person next to you. You were loved before you could ever do a single thing to earn it because he made you and wants you to know him. Jesus invites *everyone* to become part of God's family:

> *'... to all who believed [Jesus] and accepted him, he gave the right to become children of God.'* **John 1:12**

God has already turned to us and said… 'I WANT YOU'. You never have to perform to win God's love, you just need to turn to him and accept it.

Jesus was clear that we don't get to make up our own version of a creator that fits our own convenient way of thinking or our lifestyle. Maybe this was why so many people found him so controversial. He acted like he really knew God as his Father. And he challenged anyone who tried to say that we have to earn God's love. Ultimately, Jesus claimed he was more than just a man who reflected what God was like. And people would soon find out he was more than willing to die for that conviction.

'CHRIST SHOWS US EXACTLY WHAT GOD IS LIKE AND REMINDS US WHO WE REALLY ARE.'

QUESTIONS TO THINK ABOUT:

- What does the idea that Jesus shows us what God is really like mean to you?
- Where do you think most people form their view of what God is like from?
- What can we learn about God from looking at Jesus?

WATCH THIS VIDEO:

4

RESCUER?

LEARN HOW TO RECEIVE A FRESH START WITH JESUS

You only need to scroll through your newsfeed for five minutes to see that society is broken on a global scale. The headlines are full of real-life stories that could easily come straight out of a waking nightmare.

- 'Killer gets away with murder.'
- 'Politician breaks another promise.'
- 'Celebrity marriage fails.'

Then it gets worse.

- 'Children die of starvation.'
- 'Another school shooting.'
- 'War breaks out.'

It's not the fake news that gets to you; it's the real stuff that hits hard.

You'd think society ought to be better than it was in the past. We have better education, faster internet, and smarter phones. But all this technological progress doesn't seem to add up to a happier, healthier world. We can't even seem to fix our own problems even when we throw our best efforts at them.

You can try to shift the blame onto everyone else for all the bad stuff in the world – until you admit that you make mistakes, too. Everyone messes up. Nobody has a perfect track record.

Here's the thing about the big challenges we face in the world today. Is there enough wealth to go around everyone in the world? Absolutely. Is there enough food to feed everyone in the world?

100%. So, what's stopping us then? Humans are. Whether talking about topics like climate change, the destruction of the planet, the rights of children, ending war, or tackling racism, the same problem rears its ugly head. These are important issues, but they are not *the* issue. Every problem finds its root in the selfishness of the human heart. And until there's a change of heart, we will never see a change in the world.

This is not a new challenge. It's been around since day one. In the beginning, God made humans to enjoy relationships with himself and with each other. Yet from the moment Adam and Eve disobeyed God in the Garden of Eden, a story found at the start of the Bible from **Genesis 3**, it's like we have decided we could do life much better on our own.

We have *all* ghosted God. We've cut off all communication. This is way worse than being ignored after someone doesn't respond to your message straight away. We're like toddlers who rebelled against our parents and think we can look after ourselves only to end up in a total mess. This world of suffering and sadness can be traced back to the fact that we have all told God, 'We want to do it our way.'

And look where things ended up! The Bible calls this mess *sin* and we are all responsible for it.

> *'For everyone has sinned; we all fall short of God's glorious standard.'* **Romans 3:23**

When we betray, hurt, or deliberately choose not to listen to someone we love, it affects the relationship we have with them. We damage our connection. Every lie drives us further and further apart. Shame creeps in. Trust is destroyed. We become totally separated. This is exactly what has happened between God and humans.

But rather than abandoning us, God has responded by choosing to love us. The genuine hope of the Christian message is this: Jesus still changes human hearts and connects us with God again.

The problem is we don't always think we need to be rescued.

A LIFELINE WE NEED TO HOLD ON TO

I once read about the two different challenges a lifeguard faces when they are trying to save swimmers lost at sea. First there are the flappers. These swimmers get into difficulty, panic, and try everything they can to stay afloat in their own strength. When people fight, splash, and flail so hard to save themselves, they often end up exhausted by their own failed attempts. This is just like people who are trying to get out of their own mess in life, but their best efforts seem like a drop in the ocean.

Then there are the drifters. These types of swimmers don't think they need rescuing. They think everything is going swimmingly… until suddenly it's not. They haven't noticed how far they have drifted from the shoreline towards danger. By the time they realise they're in trouble, it's somctimes too late.

Jesus came for both types of people. He came to help those that know they are in trouble and can't get out of it on their own. And he came to save those that don't even realise they need saving yet. He came to rescue the entire world. Through Jesus, we find that much needed lifeline.

The good news is that God recognised we couldn't make it to the shore on our own. We could never save ourselves. An experienced rescuer can see you need help even before you see it yourself. And the cross is how Jesus rescues us.

> *'God sent his Son into the world not to judge the world, but to save the world through him.'*
> **John 3:17**

A SIGN THAT POINTS TO LOVE

So, where does the cross come into this? Nowadays, we see the image of the cross everywhere – on church steeples, around people's neck as a fashion item, on tattoos, and even in movies to ward off vampires!

If we see a swoosh, we immediately think of Nike reminding us to 'Just do it.' When we spot the Golden Arches, we instantly start wanting a burger.

And then we see a cross... but the message isn't always clear because, as a symbol, it's been so overused. For Christians, the cross is more than a fun accessory; it's a lifesaver. And the cross is not just for Christians, it's for everyone.

Perhaps the most common objection to the claims of Christianity is that our world is so messed up. Surely, if God existed, he would have stepped in and fixed it by now! When is God going to get involved?

The symbol of the cross is a reminder that God has stepped in already.

> *'There is no greater love than to lay down one's life for one's friends.'* **John 15:13**

The day Jesus died on the cross was the worst day in history. His good friend Judas betrayed him and sold his location to his enemies for a cash reward. Then, when the soldiers came to arrest him, Christ's friends scattered and left him for dead. Can you imagine your best mates turning their backs on you when you needed them most? Worse still, they even denied knowing him altogether.

Then Jesus was subject to an unfair trial where people lied through their back teeth to convict him of crimes he didn't commit. They stripped him naked, beat him up, and spat in his face. Even though the accusations were a total joke, somehow the people in charge bowed to cancel culture and sentenced him to death.

Next came the cross itself. Let's just say it was absolute torture. Whilst he was hanging on the cross, Jesus would have been visible for all to see. In that moment, he totally understood what it was like to feel like an outsider. Labelled as a criminal, his reputation lay in tatters. He was bullied, harassed, humiliated, and left out. Both the physical and emotional pain would have been unimaginable. Eventually, Christ breathed his last breath and died. It was sickening.

But thankfully, that wasn't the end of the story.

A CHANCE TO START AGAIN

The reason people love video games so much is that it gives them the opportunity to play the same challenges and scenarios over and over until they get them right and win. Make a mistake and you can simply start again.

In real life, it's not that easy. Inside each of us there is a desire to begin again, to have a do-over, and to get a fresh start. We struggle to see beyond our selfishness, our painful experiences, and our past mistakes. It feels like these cannot be undone by the simple touch of a button.

What if Jesus provides a reset?

Deep down, we all know wrongs need to be righted. Justice needs to be served. Pain needs to be healed. But all the bad stuff that has ever gone on in the world, the wrong that has happened to you and me, and the mistakes that we have made ourselves, have racked up a debt no one can repay.

Just like on social media people get banned for misusing the platform, we get banned from heaven for misusing the people and the world God has made. We'll be called to account for the way we've hurt people, for all the bad stuff we've done, and for all the good stuff we've not done.

But this is where the good news kicks in. By willingly dying on our behalf, Jesus paid a price that made the way for humankind to have their slate wiped clean. Jesus sacrificed himself to offer the chance to reset the scales for all of us. God himself takes the hit.

We might appreciate the fact that Jesus was an outstanding teacher, but God knew we needed more than an inspirational message to fix the world. Jesus didn't just tell us about God's love, he showed it. You would have to be crazy, head over heels, bonkers in love with someone to give your life for them. The cross proves that even when we throw our worst at God, God still forgives us if we turn to him. Questions about whether God loves us, or where God is in the middle of suffering, are forever answered when you look at the cross.

> *'But God showed his great love for us by sending Christ to die for us while we were still sinners.'* **Romans 5:8**

Jesus rescues us by dying for us. He swaps his goodness with our badness and faces the consequences so we don't have to. It means we can know forgiveness now, and can be sure that we won't be rejected by God, not in this life, and not after we die. We don't do anything to earn or deserve this.

What does God ask of us in return? All we need to do is receive forgiveness and a new life with him as a gift. This is the greatest act of mercy ever known. And it is summed up in one amazing word: Grace.

> *'God saved you by his grace when you believed. And you can't take credit for this; it is a gift from God.'* **Ephesians 2:8**

Grace means forgiveness and a brand-new start.

There is a scene in *The Lion King* that illustrates how God deals with us through grace when it comes to tackling our mistakes. Early in the film, King Mufasa tells the young cub Simba not to go beyond Pride Rock towards the shadows. Of course, the curious Simba ignores his father's command and takes his young friend Nala to see what it is like just beyond where the light touches the plains. Suddenly in danger in a dark cavern, they end up being ambushed by hyenas, and are almost eaten alive before Mufasa roars in at the last minute and rescues them.

After they return home, Simba is beckoned by his father and he is certain that he's about to be shouted at and shamed for what he has done. But Mufasa calmly talks to his son, expressing disappointment in his choices. He tells him exactly what he has done, the dangerous consequences, and what was at stake. There is no getting away from it. The mess was exposed. But then he restates what he, as a father, did to cover his mistake. Mufasa stepped in and dealt with the danger. There is no way Simba could have handled it on his own. He reminds Simba who he is, affirms his love, and tells him he is part of a bigger story. Forgiveness comes quickly. They finish by laughing and playing together on the hillside. A scene that should have ended in judgement ends in grace.

This is exactly how God deals with us. We never need to feel unable to come to him and say sorry when we have messed up or made mistakes. God knows it all anyway. He reminds us we are rescued and forgiven through what Jesus did on the cross and how he has dealt with the problem. Then he tells us again who we are and that we are part of a bigger story.

> *'This is real love – not that we loved God, but that he loved us and sent his Son as a sacrifice to take away our sins.'* **1 John 4:10**

When we deserve to be judged, instead, God deals with our mess and chooses a relationship with us. That's how much God loves us.

AN OFFER WE CAN'T REFUSE

There's a viral game called the Paperclip Challenge. It's where you try to upgrade a small item by swapping it with something else that's a bit better. You swap again and again, trying to end up with something really good. One time, a man called Kyle MacDonald started with a normal red paperclip and swapped it for a pen that looked like a fish. Then he traded the pen for a novelty doorknob. He kept going, making better swaps each time, even getting a real-life snowmobile – which he traded – and at one point an afternoon with a rock star. Just a year and fourteen swaps later, he ended up with a two-storey house!

Can you imagine starting with something of so little value and ending up with something worth so much? That's an incredible deal.

God, however, has an even better offer for us.

> *'We are made right with God by placing our faith in Jesus Christ. And this is true for everyone who believes, no matter who we are.'* **Romans 3:22**

This is the deal offered to you. You bring to God:

- All the times you have done things your way and ended up in a mess.
- All the mistakes you have ever made.
- All the shame and guilt you have ever felt.
- All the bad stuff that has ever been done to you by others and by the world around you.

In exchange, God will give to you a restored relationship with himself through Jesus. The benefits of this relationship include:

- All the forgiveness you will ever need from your past.
- All the comfort and peace you could ever hope for.
- All the freedom you ever want for your future.

How do you get this deal? All you have to do is ask for it. You have a problem that can only be fixed by God. This means confessing you are sorry and no longer want to do things your way. The Bible calls this 'repentance' which means 'turning around'. Ask God to help you and he promises he will.

Then you put your trust in Jesus to rescue you and you choose to follow him. The Bible word is 'faith'.

That's an offer that sounds almost too good to be true. Except it's the deal of the century… and that's why Christians call it good news.

'CHRIST SAVES US BY DYING FOR US.'

QUESTIONS TO THINK ABOUT:

- What does the idea that Jesus can rescue the world mean to you?
- What do you think we all need rescuing from?
- What do you think Jesus dying on the cross has to do with being rescued?

WATCH THIS VIDEO:

5

REVOLUTIONARY?

FIND OUT WHY JESUS REFRAMES YOUR WORLD WITH HOPE

For good or bad, the metaverse is finally here! Virtual reality is changing the way people engage with stories. We're invited to immerse ourselves into a 360-degree experience rather than just watching a screen or reading words on a page. Crazy technology allows us to teleport ourselves anywhere in the world and feel as though we're right there in the moment. Why not interact with real-life characters from history or go on a sci-fi adventure to a far-off future? Want to make an avatar that looks like a cross between a Simpsons character and Sonic the Hedgehog? You got it. You can even take a trip to the moon and be back in time for lunch!

Maybe the reason we love virtual reality so much is that we want to feel part of the story. We like the idea of being able to change the world into something new. Maybe that's because we sometimes want to escape for a while?

Thankfully, Christianity is so much more than a story to be read about in the history books. The Christian faith is an invitation to get involved, following in Jesus' footsteps to make a positive difference for others. The message is not just about fixing us as individuals; but about God reshaping the world. And boy, does our world need changing right now!

DISCOVERING FRESH HOPE

Jesus was born into a nation ruled by the Roman Empire. It was a harsh world with very little hope in it. Romans would discard unwanted babies and people with disabilities. Capital punishment was common and gladiators fought to the death to entertain crowds. The Romans viewed conquering other nations as a virtue, and millions of people were enslaved. Power and might mattered far more than compassion and care of the weak.

We may no longer live in the Roman Empire, but we still feel a deep sense of the world's cruelty today. It would be easy to feel despairing about a world full of poverty, pain, and problems, if God was not in the picture.

But something inside tells us this isn't the end of the story. Jesus promised his followers that with him there's hope and peace even in dark times;

> *'I have told you all this so that you may have peace in me. Here on earth you will have many trials and sorrows. But take heart, because I have overcome the world.'* **John 16:33**

Before *Avengers Infinity War* came out, there was so much speculation about the plot online but I was desperate to avoid any spoilers. But (spoiler alert) no one expected half the Universe to be 'blipped' out of existence by Thanos. As the end credits rolled, the original Avengers, Iron Man, Captain America, Black Widow, Thor, and a few others, were left facing the loss of so many superhero friends, including Dr Strange, Spider-Man and Black Panther. That Peter Parker and Tony Stark scene was devastating! Tragedy had befallen them and they felt totally hopeless. Darkness had won the day. Or had it?

The sequel *Avengers Endgame* became the highest grossing film of all time. Perhaps the reason it did so well is that Marvel fans were desperate to know what happened following the cliff hanger at the end of the previous instalment. Would evil win forever?

SPOILER ALERT: The Avengers saved the Universe. Thanos is dead.

You can never see that moment at the end of the first film in the same way again. Things may seem hopeless, broken, and finished, but when you know what happens next, it reframes the middle of the story. Knowing the ending changes everything.

It's the same with the good news about Jesus.

SPOILER ALERT: God saved the Universe. Jesus is alive.

> *'All praise to God, the Father of our Lord Jesus Christ. It is by his great mercy that we have been born again, because God raised Jesus Christ from the dead.'* **1 Peter 1:3**

Because Jesus died and came back to life, death is not the end of the story. Jesus will one day return and make everything right. Those who have trusted in Jesus will be made alive and perfect, inside and out. The whole world will be sorted out and life will be lived as we only dream about now. It will literally be heaven on earth. Knowing the ending changes everything. The last book of the Bible is called Revelation and it gives us an insight into the future. And in that future – God wins!

> *'Look, I am making everything new!'* **Revelation 21:5**

Everyone wants to make things better than they are. God takes this one step further and promises to *make all things new.* When the end credits finally roll, the Christian story promises us that everything will get sorted out in the endgame. Knowing this will happen one day makes us feel hopeful that things can get better now.

JOINING THE REVOLUTION

Being a Christian is not just about waiting for another day to make things better. You can see the fingerprints of Jesus impacting the world all over history.

Firstly, Jesus has affected the way people think. The concept that all human life has value and that every person is created equal finds its origin in the message of Jesus. This has shaped Western society so much that most of our modern ideas about justice, equality, and law are based on what he said. Jesus has radically shaped so many of the values we hold today such as freedom, consent, and compassion.

Secondly, Jesus has affected the way people live. Many people have a dream that involves making life better for themselves – earning loads of cash, having a nice car, getting a great job, and being in a happy relationship. This is all, well… nice. But it doesn't really make us feel satisfied. Jesus gives people a purpose bigger than just having a nice, comfortable life. We need to live for more.

The rise of 'giving' related content amongst YouTube stars like Jimmy Donaldson, AKA MrBeast, shows us how much people connect with the power of generosity. MrBeast has developed a YouTube channel full of giving money and gifts to random strangers, Uber drivers, pizza delivery guys, and other fellow streamers to make a difference to them. And fans in their millions love watching these kinds of videos. It moves us to think about changing the lives of others. We long to be able to make the world a better place. Why? Because deep inside we know we are not supposed to live just for ourselves. God has put this desire in us.

> *'God saved you by his grace when you believed. And you can't take credit for this; it is a gift from God... He has created us anew in Christ Jesus, so we can do the good things he planned for us long ago.'* **Ephesians 2:8, 10**

As we choose to follow Jesus' way and not our own, we begin to live out the purpose for which all humans were born. To live with a sense of purpose changes everything. Someone once said that the two most important days in our lives are the day we are born, and the day we find out why. Knowing our purpose motivates us, helps us keep focus when life gets tough, and empowers us to make important choices about what to do with our life, our time, and our energy.

When God changes our lives, we are invited to join a long-term revolution, first ignited by Jesus, that has been going on for 2,000 years. Jesus has been the inspiration behind the modern way of educating children, establishing universities, and building hospitals. Knowing Jesus has motivated people to start orphanages, create homes for the elderly, care for the poor, feed the hungry, and help the homeless. So many famous people in history have been inspired by Jesus. It is almost like they saw a sign of hope that said 'things can get better'. Empowered by God, they set to work…

Florence Nightingale saw that sign of hope and it changed healthcare forever. She never would have called herself religious, but one night in

1837, when she was just seventeen years old, she felt God telling her to give her life to the service of something bigger. Sick and tired of the poor treatment received by those who were sick and tired in the war, she did something about it, and now we have modern nursing.

Michael Faraday saw that sign of hope and it changed science forever. Back in the nineteenth century, he believed that God and science didn't have to be enemies. As a scientist, he was inspired to see God's world as a place that sparks curiosity and endless possibility. Without his work on magnetic fields and transmitters, we wouldn't have utilised electricity as we do, which means you would never have had the chance to scroll on your mobile phone. (Thank you, Faraday!) Oh and of course we wouldn't have lights either…

Martin Luther King Jr. saw that sign of hope and it influenced the Civil Rights Movement forever. He was angry at the unequal treatment of black people in America and organised non-violent protests whilst giving powerful speeches inspired by his love for Jesus. He was shot and killed for what he spoke against, but his words still live on today.

The list of empowered people goes on and on. But this revolution is not over; there is still more work to be done.

MAKING A DIFFERENCE

Some people think you have to be a pastor or a preacher to be useful for God, but history tells us otherwise. You don't have to be the smartest or the strongest person in the room, you just have to be available. There are so many breakthroughs that have come through ordinary people motivated by Jesus. Many of these world changers were teenagers, and they were all sold out on the idea of hope.

Leaders often try to gain power to use it for their own benefit. Everything is about building a bigger platform so they can get more privilege and position. They want to be served rather than to serve. But Jesus was not like this at all.

'For even the Son of Man [Jesus] came not to be served but to serve others and to give his life as a ransom for many.' **Matthew 20:28**

There was no doubt that Christ had power. He could heal others, perform miracles, and even raise the dead. He knew exactly what was going on in hearts and minds, and could have easily manipulated people to get what he wanted. Yet, he used his authority, gifts, and talents to benefit others. And God encourages us to do the same.

So how could you put your God-given talents to good use? The really great thing is that God doesn't want us to be robots who act the same as everyone else. There are so many ways you can follow in Jesus' footsteps in a unique way because of who he has created you to be.

'For we are God's masterpiece. He has created us anew in Christ Jesus, so we can do the good things he planned for us long ago.' **Ephesians 2:10**

Here are some quick questions you can ask to help you figure out where you can immerse yourself in making a difference:

- What am I good at? Or what do others say I am good at if I struggle to figure that out for myself?
- What am I passionate about?
- What makes me mad or sad about the world around me?
- What are my goals for the future?

Take the answers to these questions and think how you might use this all to serve and help other people, just like Jesus did. If you find it hard to figure them out, then a good idea is to chat it through with someone you trust. Two heads are always better than one!

START WHERE YOU ARE

You don't have to jump on a plane and visit some far-off corner of the world to make an impact. With God's help, we can make a difference through our home, our school, our work, and our neighbourhoods right where we are.

Want to know where to start? Jesus helped by giving us this mission statement for our life:

> *'And you must love the* LORD *your God with all your heart, all your soul, all your mind, and all your strength.' The second is equally important: 'Love your neighbour as yourself.' No other commandment is greater than these.'* **Mark 12:30–31**

You will notice here that our love for others flows out of our love for God. This is the heart of the adventure that God wants to immerse us in. Start by showing care to the person right next to you. Who knows where it could end up?

Changing the world can seem like a massive task but it starts by loving your neighbour in small ways every single day. This may look like:

- Serving others in your community.
- Training in a job or career you know can help others or improve the world.
- Becoming passionate about an issue of social justice.
- Being welcoming to those who are different from you.

- Giving your money, food, or resources to those in need.
- Visiting someone who is sick.
- Talking to a lonely person at school or college.
- Standing up for someone being bullied by telling the right person and making sure they are safe.
- Cleaning up your neighbourhood.
- Practicing listening to others.
- Dropping someone an encouraging message.
- Refusing to take part in gossip or negative talk about others.
- Mentoring or coaching someone in a skill you have.
- Doing a household chore without being asked.

The ultimate way we can show love to others is by introducing them to Jesus. When we tell others what we know about Christ, it can unlock hope in those who feel like they have none.

For those that believe that the world is broken forever, we can remind them that Jesus tells a better story.

The list of ways to be a *sign of hope* is endless... This is not meant to be just a one-time event but a lifestyle of love. As we love our neighbour, the world can change for the better.

Martin Luther King Jr. once prayed a prayer that we might want to borrow for ourselves:

> *'Use me, God. Show me how to take who I am, who I want to be, and what I can do, and use it for a purpose greater than myself.'*

Change starts when we make ourselves available.

Only with God's help can we look forward to a day when all that is broken will be made new again. And we don't have to wait till tomorrow for it to begin. Whilst we ourselves are never the rescuers, we get to introduce others to the one who rescued us.

Now that all sounds like a lifestyle, not to try to virtually escape from, but one really worth living for.

> 'WE ARE INVITED TO JOIN CHRIST'S PURPOSE TO BRING HOPE.'

QUESTIONS TO THINK ABOUT:

- What does the idea that Jesus has revolutionised the world mean to you?
- Where can we see the positive influence of Jesus in the world today?
- How does Jesus inspire you to make a difference?

WATCH THIS VIDEO:

6

RELATIONSHIP?

DISCOVER WAYS YOU CAN CONNECT WITH JESUS

A top university study discovered one major problem that can shorten your lifespan more than smoking fifteen cigarettes a day.[5] Despite being so widespread, there are no easy ways to diagnose, prevent, or even treat it. The biggest potential health crisis facing young people

5 Michele M Kroll, 'Prolonged Social Isolation and Loneliness are the Equivalent to Smoking 15 Cigarettes a Day', (3 May 2022), *University of New Hampshire*, https://bit.ly/3PRbA1d [accessed 28 June 2023]

today can't be diagnosed by checking vital signs, taking an X-ray, or testing for a virus. What is this mystery issue we are talking about? The Latin term for it would be *solitudinem*, but you and I would simply call it loneliness.

There's a big difference between being on your own and feeling alone. Physical distance sometimes means nothing… you can be three feet from another human being but feel a million miles away. Or you can go without seeing another person for days and yet still feel part of a community. You might be in a crowd and feel you are the only person in the world.

When we feel lonely, it can trigger anxiety, lower self-confidence, increase stress, and even give us problems sleeping. We feel like no one understands us, others don't really care about us, and probably won't be there for us. This can then affect our study, our work, and our relationships.

Some teenagers deal with this ache by trying to get more followers on Instagram, millions of views on TikTok, or endless messages on Snapchat. But likes don't last! We are the most technologically connected generation that has ever existed; and yet we have never felt more disconnected. Everyone loves the social buzz of interacting online, but when things get tough in real life, we need to know someone has our back IRL.

Many young people will reinvent themselves repeatedly to get the approval of as many so-called 'friends' as possible. Or they zoom in on that one special person, becoming obsessed and intoxicated by the love of their life, only to discover they're not as perfect as they first seemed. Then it all fizzles out just as quickly as it began. Before you know it, that empty feeling creeps back in again. Others fill their schedules with social events, sports teams, and busyness. Yet the party is eventually over.

Why does loneliness feel so bad that we would do anything to avoid the sensation? Because life is defined by the quality of our relationships. After all, it's not what you know, but who you know that matters.

DISCOVERING GOD IS WITH US

As Jesus' friends watched him die on the cross, they knew all too well what it was like to experience feeling alone. Having spent time with this incredible person for three years, their world was thrown into chaos when he was suddenly and brutally taken away from them. Yet despite this awful chapter, it wasn't the end of their story.

Eyewitnesses made the incredible claim that Jesus didn't stay dead! Just three days after dying on a cross, he came back to life. This was announced by an angel who appeared to a few followers who went to his empty tomb:

> *'Don't be alarmed. You are looking for Jesus of Nazareth, who was crucified. He isn't here! He is risen from the dead! Look, this is where they laid his body.'* **Mark 16:6**

People then saw Jesus again all over the place. After a period of being together, physically in person, Jesus went back up to heaven. But he left them with a promise that he would be with them in spirit wherever they go:

'And be sure of this: I am with you always, even to the end of the age.' **Matthew 28:20**

- When they faced a storm, Jesus would be there.
- When they didn't know what to do, Jesus would be there.
- When they needed a friend, Jesus would be there.

So how can Jesus be here in his spirit but not physically in his body? To answer this, we need to introduce a core belief of Christianity and explain the words *Holy Spirit*. Think of the Holy Spirit like the 'Spirit of Jesus' with you every day. The word *Holy* simply means special, and the word *Spirit* means he's spiritual not physical, so we can't see him.

Jesus is still present and at work in our world today through his Spirit. The Holy Spirit is with us all the time if we're followers of Jesus, and as the Spirit of Jesus, he brings exactly the same love, peace, power, and joy that Jesus shared with people when he physically walked on earth.

The Holy Spirit is our advocate. An advocate is someone who supports you when you are in need and stands up for you when you are in trouble.

> *'But in fact, it is best for you that I go away, because if I don't, the Advocate won't come. If I do go away, then I will send him to you.'* **John 16:7**

> *'He is the Holy Spirit, who leads into all truth.'* **John 14:17**

Even though they had spent time with him for three years, God knew that a memory or a message wasn't enough to see his friends through the challenges that were to come. Jesus knew we needed the Holy Spirit to help us because we wouldn't be able to make it in our own strength.

FINDING HELP WHEN YOU NEED IT

If I asked you to climb something like Mount Everest on your own with no preparation or support, then you would probably freak out. Rightly so! But if I said I was going to send the world-famous adventurer Bear Grylls with you as your guide, you would definitely see things differently. Having him walk side-by-side with you, and talk you through each step of the journey, would change your entire outlook on any difficult expedition. You may not know what you are doing, but the expert does. This is exactly what it's like to have Jesus as your guide for life.

In fact, Bear Grylls himself talks about the strength he found when he realised God was his true guide:

> *'This really is the heart of what I found as a young teenager: Christ comes to make us free, to bring us life in all its fullness. He is there to forgive us where we have messed up (and who hasn't), and to be the backbone in our being.'*[6]

Having a personal connection with God is not a superpower that makes you invincible. God is not a genie in a bottle, ready to answer your every wish. There's no guarantee that you will live problem free or that all your issues will be resolved overnight. Nor is it like having Santa on speed dial. It is more like knowing that a friend

---

6 Bear Grylls, *Mud, Sweat and Tears* (Channel 4 Books: 2012), p. 94.

will be with you in both the good and bad times. You are never alone again. Jesus said:

> *'But when the Father sends the Advocate as my representative – that is, the Holy Spirit – he will teach you everything and will remind you of everything I have told you.'* **John 14:26**

What keeps us going when life gets tough and challenging? What is it that causes some people to survive impossible odds whilst other people fall apart when their Wi-Fi goes down? It's often the difference between those who realise Jesus is with them and those who don't.

Let me share one example with you.

There was a man called Louis Zamperini who lived through World War II. He knew what it was like to face the trials of life. Starting his career as an American athlete, Zamperini was hailed as a hero, and he even raced against the Germans in front of Adolf Hitler at the Olympic Games in 1936. Everything seemed like it was going great for him.

Soon afterwards, he became a fighter pilot, but accidentally crashed his plane in the ocean and was stranded at sea for forty-seven days on a raft. Living without food or water, he was surrounded by sharks, shot at by Japanese planes, and constantly on the verge of death. He was then captured as a prisoner of war and kept in horrible conditions for years.

When he was finally released, Louis found out that everyone back home thought he had died years ago. This led him to try to cope with the pain and trauma by drinking more and more alcohol. He had nightmares every night and could not forgive the people that captured and tortured him.

What made the difference for Louis? One day he went to a big stadium event and heard a man called Billy Graham share a life-changing message about Jesus. This message transformed his life forever.

Zamperini became an inspiration to millions around the world with his story of forgiveness, faith, and triumph over adversity. He understood that Jesus was with him, in good times and bad. This is what it means to know God is with you. Life is not always easy – but knowing Jesus reframes everything.

HOW TO CONNECT WITH JESUS

It seems odd to think that you can have a relationship with Jesus when you can't see him. So, let's think about four points that help us develop any type of close friendship:

1. You can talk to them.
2. You can find out more about them.
3. You can spend time with their family.
4. You can act in a way that shows you value them.

Now let's apply that to how you might build a relationship with Jesus Christ.

1: TALK TO JESUS

Try praying. The Holy Spirit helps us connect with Jesus as we pray.

In the middle of the global pandemic, online searches for 'how to pray' went through the roof. But prayer is not just for when you're in a major crisis. You can talk to God about everything.

> *'Don't worry about anything; instead, pray about everything. Tell God what you need, and thank him for all he has done. Then you will experience God's peace, which exceeds anything we can understand. His peace will guard your hearts and minds as you live in Christ Jesus.'* **Philippians 4:6–7**

Prayer is simply talking to God out loud or in your head. You don't have to use any kind of special religious language or lyrics to pray, just share what's on your mind. In any of our relationships, we communicate by both talking and listening. When you really understand how much God loves you, it makes you want to say thank you. Starting with gratitude makes all the difference. Try it today!

2: FIND OUT MORE ABOUT JESUS

Read the Bible. The Holy Spirit helps us connect with Jesus as we read.

The Bible was written by forty different authors over 1,500 years, yet it is a remarkably joined up story. God has been talking about his love for humans since the beginning of time. It's not always easy to know where to start, but try reading about Jesus in the section called the New Testament.

Everything in the Bible points to Jesus – not just in the New Testament but in the Old Testament too. Jesus said that the whole Bible is one big signpost pointing to him. You can literally spend a lifetime making powerful connections with every picture, symbol, illustration, or idea that points to Christ.

One of England's favourite football players, Bukayo Saka, has shared regularly about the inspiration he finds in the Bible. In one of the Qatar 2022 World Cup press conferences, Saka said this about what the Bible means to him:

> *'I read my Bible every night. For me, it's really important to have the presence of God in me all the time and it gives me more confidence to*

know that God's plan is perfect, so I can go on the pitch and know that God has my back.'

In a world where people so often don't know what to trust, God offers timeless wisdom and truth that helps people know where to turn.

'Your word is a lamp to my feet and a light to my path.' **Psalm 119:105**

There are so many ways to read or listen to the Bible and you don't have to tackle it all in one go. Download an audio version or an App such as the *YouVersion Bible* so you can listen on your smartphone. You can make notes in a journal or scribble in the margins of your Bible to help you remember what you read. The more you read, the more it changes your life.

3: SPEND TIME WITH GOD'S FAMILY

Connect with a church community. The Holy Spirit helps us connect with Jesus through others.

You don't have to look far to find someone who has had their life changed by God. If you chat to a Christian, you will soon discover why so many choose to believe and follow Jesus. This can help you make a quality decision for yourself. Having a role model can be one of the greatest ways to grow in faith. They can actually teach you up close and personal how to live well and tackle the challenges of life. On the days when things get hard, which they inevitably do, it's important to have someone to look up to.

The church is still the best place to find Christians who are trying to follow Jesus. A church is not a building you go to but a community you belong to. Jesus promised that he would always be present when people gather together:

> *'For where two or three gather together as my followers, I am there among them.'* **Matthew 18:20**

There are as many church meeting styles as there are flavours of ice cream, but look for a local one that gets you plugged in through the Bible, teaching, and community. You can normally check out the vibe on a church website ahead of visiting. Watch YouTube videos of talks or view meetings online beforehand to figure out what it will be like. This makes it a little easier to get over the nerves of visiting a new place for the first time.

If you already know a Christian, see if you can pay a visit to their church meeting. Ideally, find somewhere that has a group of young people like you. But it's helpful to connect with people of all ages too. It might feel awkward at first. You may have to try something new, but finding a safe space in a church community is one of the greatest ways to grow in your faith.

4: ACT MORE LIKE JESUS

Practise loving others. The Holy Spirit helps us connect with Jesus through serving.

If you care about someone, you want to live in a way that pleases them. The more you spend time with a friend, the more you become like them. Jesus dedicated his life to helping, supporting, caring, and loving others. We can follow his example and do the same. And this causes us to grow in kindness and compassion. Jesus said:

'This is my commandment: Love each other in the same way I have loved you.' **John 15:12**

As we follow the commandment to love other people it changes everything. This doesn't earn us God's love – nothing can do that – but it helps position us to connect more deeply with God.

Here's a reminder of four ways we can connect with Christ.

1. Try praying.
2. Read the Bible.
3. Connect with a church community.
4. Act more like Jesus.

The heart of Christ's message was that we are all loved children who find identity and purpose when we discover *God is with us.* This was why his followers were so full of hope and courage – they knew they were not alone anymore.

Every time you talk to Jesus, find out more about him, spend time with God's family, or live your life in a way that follows Christ's example, you can know the reality of God being with you.

And because of Jesus, no matter what you'll face, you never have to be alone again.

'WHEN YOU PUT YOUR TRUST IN CHRIST, HE WILL BE WITH YOU FOREVER.'

QUESTIONS TO THINK ABOUT:

- What does the idea that we can have a relationship with God mean to you?
- What are some ways you know people connect with God?
- What will you do because of your experience learning about Jesus?

WATCH THIS VIDEO:

7

RESET?

WHAT EVERY TEENAGER NEEDS TO DECIDE ABOUT JESUS

There are many people who seem to be searching for something but they don't quite know what it is. I believe Jesus provides the answer to the thirst of every heart.

- Looking for satisfaction? Christ provides us with what we are really looking for. Jesus is relevant.

- Looking for truth? History proves that Christ was a real person who made a real difference. Jesus is real.
- Looking for identity? Christ shows us exactly what God is like and reminds us who we really are. Jesus is God's reflection.
- Looking for forgiveness? Christ saves us by dying for us. Jesus is a rescuer.
- Looking for purpose? We are invited to join Christ's purpose to bring hope. Jesus is a revolutionary.
- Looking to feel close? When you put your trust in Christ, he will be with you forever. Jesus offers you a relationship.

Whatever you end up believing about Jesus, there is no doubt that so many people are never the same after they find him. What if it is time for your reset moment?

Here are three options for what to do next.

OPTION 1: UNSUBSCRIBE

Unsubscribing is what we do when we don't want to receive further notifications or information. At some point we all need to decide whether to say 'yes' or to say 'no' to Jesus. We can't sit on the fence forever. It might be that you've decided to say 'no' to Jesus. That's a big thing, but respect that you have taken time to check it all out first. So many people don't even bother to get this far.

But before you totally disengage from Jesus and check out, it's worth asking yourself the following questions:

- What makes you want to unsubscribe? Is this something you might change your mind about in the future?
- Is there anything you want to know more about before you leave it for now?
- What are you saying 'no' to?
- Why do you think other people might want to know more?

If unsubscribing is genuinely where you are at now but later you change your mind, you can always sign up again at a later date. But with a decision this significant, it might be that you feel it's worth sticking around for a bit longer.

OPTION 2: LIKE

You may like some of what you have read but are not quite ready to go all in. Here are a few ideas for you to consider next:

- Is there a person you could talk to, to explore more?
- What about reading one of the four eyewitness accounts in the Bible? I would go for the book of Mark first as it's the shortest.
- You could make a list of all Jesus' personality traits. What's he like? How did he treat people? What might this tell you about what God is like?
- What would it feel like to know you are forgiven with a clean slate? Imagine the benefits of a fresh start and consider if there's someone better than Jesus who can offer you one.

- Think of ways you want to make a difference in the world. How might exploring more about Christianity help motivate you to do this?
- Pick one way to experience connecting with God. Try praying or visiting a church. See what happens!

Thank you for your willingness to remain open-minded.

OPTION 3: FOLLOW

Think about this: Who we choose to copy can actually change the course of our life. Because it's not just fashion that we copy, but our role models' attitudes, goals, and behaviour as well.

BEING A CHRISTIAN IS ABOUT CHOOSING TO FOLLOW JESUS.

We want to imitate our heroes in what they say and do, and how they see life. Yet how many of our so-called role models are actually living a dream that could turn into a nightmare if we really followed it through? We so often hear celebrities who are at the top of their game say how unhappy they are on the inside. Why would someone follow them?

This is where Jesus shows us that life is about more than getting rich, famous, and making sure you are the most important and beautiful person at the party. Life is about having a rock-solid relationship with your Creator and finding his purpose for you. You can trust Jesus completely. He will never let you down as he leads you.

There is this thing called fangirling. Apparently, you can do it even if you are a guy! It is the over-the-top reaction of a fan to any mention or sighting of their favourite celebrity. These reactions often include shortness of breath, fainting, high-pitched noises, shaking, awkward selfies, and intense blogging. They kind of sound like side effects of a prescription medication.

And when you get two fangirls together, then an endless amount of energy will be wasted on discussing, arguing, and cyber-stalking their flavour of the month. Fangirling can take over your life. If a celebrity goes out in a blue dress, the next day every fan in the modern world does the same. After all, how can you be original unless you copy everyone else?

Fangirling isn't really the same as following though because it's based on feeling excited all the time. What happens when the going gets tough or the person you are imitating does something that goes against your preference? What do you do when the trend changes or the crowd moves on?

Jesus doesn't say for us to *follow* in the way social media means follow. It doesn't mean all that much if you say you are a follower of someone online. You don't really know them. You don't have to commit to anything or change your life in response to being near them. But Jesus expected people's allegiance – to get up and go with him, wherever he leads.

> *'As Jesus was walking along, he saw a man named Matthew sitting at his tax collector's booth. "Follow me and be my disciple," Jesus said to him. So Matthew got up and followed him.'* **Matthew 9:9**

Jesus said, 'Follow me', and then took people on a journey to be his apprentices or 'disciples'. A disciple is someone who tries to put what they learn into practice every day.

- We follow Jesus when we listen to his words.
- We follow Jesus when we think more like him.
- We follow Jesus when we imitate his actions.

Years ago, I had a go at white water rafting. When the instructor started talking and teaching us, I hung on every word he said. I had barely met the guy, but I listened as if my life depended on it. Why? Because in a few short minutes, I would have to do what he instructed me about for real. You don't want to be out on a roaring river and not know how to use a paddle.

Listening matters when you know you have to put it into practice. Being a disciple means learning as if your life depended on it. You may have heard Jesus say things like 'Love your neighbour' or 'Forgive others'. But as a disciple, you're actually going to live it out yourself.

> *'Jesus said to the people who believed in him, "You are truly my disciples if you remain faithful to my teachings. And you will know the truth, and the truth will set you free."'* **John 8:31–32**

It may seem restrictive to only do what God tells us to, but the opposite is true. When we follow the instructions of our Maker everything fits into place. There's a promise of freedom when we start to put what Jesus says into practice. It all starts with a decision to listen to your instructor.

A PRAYER TO FINISH

Prayer is simply talking to God. It is not a magic wish. It doesn't solve all your problems overnight. But it's amazing that God wants to hear what's on our hearts and minds. We can pray to God and tell him we want in. If you turn to Jesus, you can know you're so loved by God. You can know you're so forgiven by God. You can know God has a plan for your life. When the world says you are useless, you can know God says you are worth something.

If you want to decide to follow Jesus today then this verse tells you how:

> *'If you openly declare that Jesus is Lord and believe in your heart that God raised him from the dead, you will be saved. For it is by believing in your heart that you are made right with God, and it is by openly declaring your faith that you are saved.'* **Romans 10:9–10**

According to this Bible passage, for a person to be ready to follow Jesus, they simply need to remember their ABCs:

- Admit that they need Jesus Christ.
- Believe what Jesus Christ has done for them through his life, death, and resurrection.
- Confess their faith before God and others.

Therefore, when I think about praying to help take the first steps with God, I always think about the words a mum teaches her child to say when they are young… *Thank you! Sorry! Please!*

You may want to quietly pray something like this:

- *Say thank you.* Thank you, Jesus – for making me, loving me, and dying for me to bring me back into a relationship with you.
- *Say sorry.* Sorry, Jesus – for messing up and living life on my agenda and by my own rules.
- Say *please.* Please Jesus, come and rescue me, become the leader of my life, heal me from my past. Help me live for you and walk with me every step of the way.

If you decide to pray this kind of prayer, then ideally, if you know a Christian, chat to them about what you have read. Here's an incredible promise for you about the fresh start you can now have with Jesus:

> *'This means that anyone who belongs to Christ has become a new person. The old life is gone; a new life has begun!'* **2 Corinthians 5:17**

For over 2,000 years, Jesus has been changing lives and transforming our world for the better. In the past, God has used ordinary teenagers to do incredible things and he can do it again with you. It doesn't matter who you are, what you've done, or where you've been. When you say yes to following Jesus, you say yes to a life that could take you places you never could have imagined. Why not dare to dream? You say yes to life with him, now and forever, knowing Jesus has rescued you now and forever.

NOW IS THE TIME FOR YOUR ADVENTURE TO BEGIN!